Letter Carriers
Community Workers

by Alice K. Flanagan

Content Adviser: Candace Main Rush,
Information Center, National Association of Letter Carriers

Reading Adviser: Dr. Linda D. Labbo,
Department of Reading Education, College of Education,
The University of Georgia

COMPASS POINT BOOKS

Minneapolis, Minnesota

Compass Point Books
3722 West 50th Street, #115
Minneapolis, MN 55410

Visit Compass Point Books on the Internet at *www.compasspointbooks.com* or e-mail your request to *custserv@compasspointbooks.com*

Photographs ©:

FPG International/Dick Luria, cover; Photri-Microstock/B. Jones, 4; Unicorn Stock Photos/Aneal Vohra, 5; International Stock/ Mark Gibson, 6; David F. Clobes, 7; FPG International/Tom Tracy, 8; FPG International/Denis Scott, 10; FPG International/ Bill Losh, 11; Unicorn Stock Photos/Gerry Schnieders, 12; Visuals Unlimited/Jeff Greenberg, 13; FPG International/Dick Luria, 14; International Stock/Bill Stanton, 15; David F. Clobes, 16; Photri-Microstock/Bachmann, 17; David F. Clobes, 18; David F. Clobes, 20; Leslie O'Shaughnessy, 21; David F. Clobes, 22; FPG International/Dick Luria, 24; FPG International/Bill Losh, 26; David F. Clobes, 27.

Editors: E. Russell Primm and Emily J. Dolbear
Photo Researcher: Svetlana Zhurkina
Photo Selector: Linda S. Koutris
Design: Bradfordesign, Inc.

Library of Congress Cataloging-in-Publication Data

Flanagan, Alice K.
     Letter carriers / by Alice K. Flanagan.
          p. cm. — (Community workers)
     Includes bibliographical references and index.
     Summary: Introduces the job of letter carrier, including the duties, skills, physical requirements, uniforms, and contribution to the community.
     ISBN 0-7565-0010-9
          1. Letter carriers—United States—Juvenile literature. [1. Letter carriers. 2. Occupations.]
I. Title. II. Series.
     HE6499 .F55 2000
     383'.145'02373—dc21

00-008626

Table of Contents

What Do Letter Carriers Do?

Letter carriers collect and deliver our mail. Letter carriers walk or drive to the area where they deliver the mail. Six days a week they deliver mail along the same streets. Those streets are called **routes**.

◀ A letter carrier on her route

A letter carrier delivers mail from a mail truck. ▶

What Tools and Equipment Do They Use?

At the beginning of each day, letter carriers **sort** the mail using a big **case**. The case has one slot for each address. A case holds letters, bills, magazines, packages, and **ads** from stores. Then the letter carriers put the mail in long, plastic trays. They then carry the trays to their trucks.

◀ Sorting the mail

Carrying trays of mail to ▶
the truck

Some letter carriers walk along their routes. They carry the mail in **satchels** on their shoulders or in a cart with wheels.

A letter carrier puts mail through a door slot.

How Do Letter Carriers Help?

We count on letter carriers to deliver important letters and packages. Letter carriers meet many people on their routes. Sometimes the letter carrier sees people at home who are in trouble and calls for help.

◀ Letter carriers meet people of all ages in the neighborhood.

A letter carrier gets to know the people on the route. ▶

Where Do They Work?

Letter carriers deliver mail in every city and small town. Sometimes they have to deliver it to places that are hard to get to, such as mountain cabins or farms in the country.

◀ Delivering mail in the country

A small rural post office ▶

Who Do They Work With?

Most of the people letter carriers work with are the people on their routes. Sometimes, letter carriers deliver mail to office buildings.

◀ Delivering mail to a house

A letter carrier ▶
in the city

What Do They Wear?

Letter carriers wear blue **uniforms** and shoes that are good for walking. In winter, letter carriers wear warm clothing. In summer, they wear shorts and a hat that protects them from the sun.

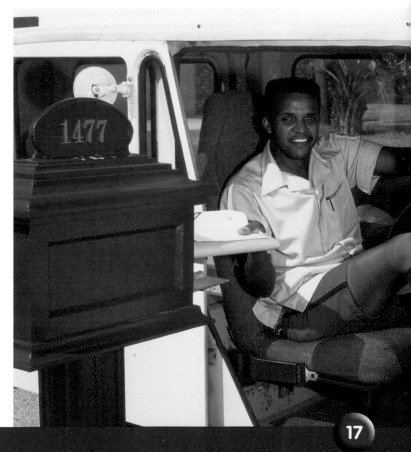

◄ A letter carrier wears a warm uniform and boots in the winter.

Shorts and short-sleeved shirts are the summer uniform ►

What Training Does It Take?

People who want to be letter carriers must finish high school. They must pass a test to see if they have the right skills to be a letter carrier. Then letter carriers who have done the job for years will teach them how to deliver mail.

◀ Letter carriers sort mail at the post office.

What Skills Do They Need?

Letter carriers should read very well and be good at math. They should also have a good memory and be able to sort the mail. On the job, they work with names, numbers, and directions.

A letter carrier must be able to read addresses and sort mail quickly.

This letter carrier ▶ makes sure letters go into the right mail box.

What Problems Do They Face?

Delivering mail is hard work. Letter carriers lift and carry heavy loads. They walk many miles in all kinds of weather. Even if it is raining or snowing, letter carriers must deliver the mail. Sometimes, they have to deal with barking dogs.

Sometimes letter carriers make friends with the dogs on their routes.

Would You Like to Be a Letter Carrier?

Do you like people? Do you like walking and being outside? Maybe you would like to be a letter carrier someday. You can prepare now. In school, learn how to follow directions. Talk to people and be friendly. Be someone others can count on.

◀ A letter carrier should enjoy working with people.

A Letter Carrier's Tools and Clothes

hat

letters

shirt

satchel

pants

shoes

At the Post Office

sorted mail

uniform

desk

letters

sorting box

cart

A Letter Carrier's Day

Early morning
- The letter carrier arrives at the post office very early in the morning.
- First, the letter carrier sorts the day's mail with the other letter carriers.
- He also places notes in the case to remind him about special letters or packages.

Noon
- The letter carrier puts the mail for the route in his cart.
- Then, he starts his route, walking with his cart.
- He delivers mail to people's home mailboxes.
- Sometimes, he has to get a person to sign for a letter or package.

Afternoon
- On his route, he stops to say hello to a disabled woman who works at home.
- He also takes mail to be sent from mailboxes along the route.

Evening
- After the mail is delivered, the letter carrier takes the mail to be sent back to the post office.

Night
- He has to get to bed, because he delivers the mail on Saturdays too!

Glossary

ads—printed information about items for sale

case—a box for holding things

routes—the streets that a letter carrier delivers mail to every day

satchels—small bags with a shoulder strap

sort—arrange the mail into groups

uniforms—clothes worn by members of a group

Did You Know?

- The U.S. Postal Service delivers 630 million pieces of mail a day.

- The U.S. Postal Service delivers 41 percent of all the mail in the world.

- About 332,000 letter carriers work for the U.S. Postal Service.

Want to Know More?

At the Library

Burns, Peggy. *The Mail*. New York: Thomson Learning, 1995.

Flanagan, Alice K., and Christine Osinkski (photographer). *Here Comes Mr. Eventoff with the Mail!* Danbury, Conn.: Children's Press, 1998.

Skurzynski, Gloria. *Here Comes the Mail*. New York: Bradbury Press, 1992.

On the Web

Smithsonian National Postal Museum

http://www.si.edu/postal/

Information about this museum, which is part of the Smithsonian complex

The U.S. Postal Service (USPS)

http://www.usps.gov/

The official site of the USPS

Through the Mail

U.S. Postal Service

Public and Employee Communications Department

Washington, DC 20260

For information on working for the U.S. Postal Service

On the Road

National Postal Museum

2 Massachusetts Avenue, N.E.

Washington, DC 20002

202/633-9360

For the history of the postage stamp

Index

About the Author
Alice K. Flanagan writes books for children and teachers. Since she was a young girl, she has enjoyed writing. Today, she has published more than seventy books on a wide variety of topics. Some of the books she has written include biographies of U.S. presidents and first ladies; biographies of people working in neighborhoods; phonics books for beginning readers; informational books about birds and Native Americans; and career education in the classroom. Alice K. Flanagan lives in Chicago, Illinois.